Rainbow trout hooked on a #4 Black Bunny Leech, King Salmon Creek, Alaska.

Landing a rainbow, Yellowstone River, Yellowstone National Park, Wyoming.

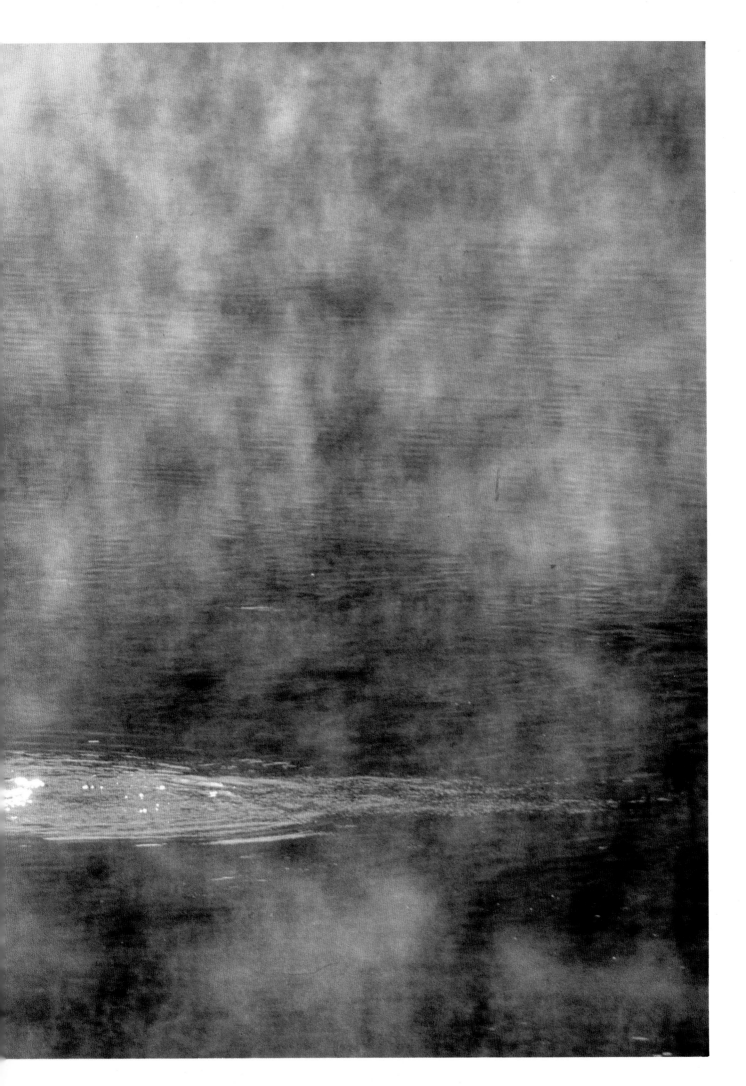

Casting for tarpon, Islamorada, Florida.

Fishing for brook trout on a beaver pond, Big Wood River, Montana.

Netting a rainbow, Loving Creek, Idaho.

Published by Thomasson-Grant, Inc.: Frank L. Thomasson III and John F. Grant, Directors;
C. Douglas Elliott, Product Development; Carolyn M. Clark, Creative Director; Mary Alice Parsons, Art Director;
Hoke Perkins, Senior Editor; Jim Gibson, Production Manager.

Designed by Leonard G. Phillips
Edited by Hoke Perkins

Any inquiries should be directed to Thomasson-Grant, Inc.,
One Morton Drive, Suite 500, Charlottesville, Virginia 22901, telephone (804) 977-1780.
ISBN 0-934738-50-5
Library of Congress Cataloging-in-Publication Data

Rosenbauer, Tom.
Casting illusions.

1. Fly fishing. I. Title.
SH456.R65   1989   799.1'2   88-4053

Casting ILLUSIONS

THE WORLD OF FLY-FISHING

TEXT BY TOM ROSENBAUER

THOMASSON-GRANT
Charlottesville, Virginia

Milton Lake, California.

The Ausable River in upstate New York is not a place that anyone enjoys on a mid-June evening, unless he is interested in observing one of the meanest populations of black flies outside of the North Woods, so thick they break through defenses of wool, netting, insect repellent, and pipe smoke. Yet three people have just stepped into the river, dressed in baggy waders. They space themselves 100 yards apart in a long, riffly pool, and in the evening mist, their only clues to each other's presence are fuzzy forms that could be tree trunks along the riverbank.

Upstream, in the head of the riffle, stands a 63-year-old man who could be mistaken for nothing but a local. He has seen the moods of this river for as long as he can remember, and can tell stories that stretch back into the last century, passed on to him by his father, who, in between guiding city sports to brook trout, deer, and bear, taught the old man how to fish. He holds a fly rod that he bought in a hardware store decades ago, and although it practically creaks in protest of the thousands of flexes it has endured, the old strips of bamboo serve him well.

The man's casting is barely adequate: despite the gentle prodding of younger friends, he has never bothered to improve his timing. Like the rod, his skill is just enough. Nor does he bother trying to identify or imitate the mayflies starting to twitch from the river, prompting the trout to feed on the surface with sounds that remind him of his two-year-old grandson kissing a teddy bear. He almost always fishes with a single fly pattern, a local favorite called the Haystack, a coarse, buggy fly made from deer hair and fox fur that is sinfully attractive to trout. In fact, he has been fishing every evening for a week and has never clipped the fly off his leader; he just chucks the rod into the back of his pickup at each day's end.

The sun slips behind the sharp granite edges of Wilmington Notch. All traces of evening breezes vanish. The smell of balsam heralds a fresh hatch of mayflies. One hundred yards below the old man, a much younger man is ready. He knows exactly which species of mayfly is hatching—*Ephemera guttulatta*, called Green Drakes by fishermen. He has a perfect imitation of the fly, tied months before in the dark hours of a Connecticut winter. His vest is neat. His waders are new. His rod is made from the latest generation of aerospace fiber, and although

his casting is not much better than the old man's, it will improve with time, because this young man approaches everything in his life with the same fervor as he does his job as an investment counselor.

The old man above him could not tell you why he fishes with a fly or even why he came to the river tonight. Something in the air, something he smelled or tasted or sensed, told him it was a night for good fishing, just as his father could sense where a buck would be at first light. The young man, on the other hand, fishes here because the books he read told him that the Green Drakes would be hatching on this date, just before dark, in slow pools with silt bottoms and in the sandy patches behind fat boulders in the tumbling pocket water.

And he could tell you why fly-fishing appealed to him so much that it became an obsession.

The pressures of his job had invaded every second of his life. He needed a release and had tried paddle tennis, golf, windsurfing—and then, on a friend's suggestion, a fly-fishing school. As soon as he stepped into a trout stream, his mind was washed clean of worries. The intellectual challenges were constant, and even when he could figure out a small piece of the puzzle, the layer upon layer of variables that a dynamic system like a trout stream could introduce brought him right back to square one. Nothing was ever the same two days in a row: water temperature, the species of fly that was hatching, what fly the fish took best. Even as he watched a single square foot of water, the currents would pitch and yaw and surround each pebble with an ever-changing necklace of silver bubbles.

A couple of times he even tried to think about work while he was fishing, just to test his self-prescribed therapy. Not a chance.

This evening he concentrates on wading the Ausable's tricky currents; they tug at his legs, threatening to upend him should he let his mind wander. He searches the water for mayflies, and when he spots a few, begins to look for rising trout. Glimpsing one, he tries to tie on a fly while watching out of the corner of his eye for another rise. Next, he casts, keeping the fly in the air just behind the trout until he gauges the distance, then shoots line on the last cast to drop the fly two feet above the fish. But the fly drags, pulled by the line and leader over currents of varying speed, and the

trout shows no interest in this insect that does not behave naturally. He casts 20 more times with no luck.

Now the game begins in earnest. Is the fly the wrong pattern? Maybe his leader is too heavy. Should he change positions, getting a casting angle that will lessen the drag on the fly, or will moving around startle the trout and stop it from feeding? He even considers looking for another feeding fish that might not be as hard to catch. But no, he will stay with this one until he hooks it or spooks it, even if he must fish into darkness, relying on sound and a fading sliver of moon to tell him the trout is still feeding.

The young man is oblivious to everything but that fish. He does not feel the slight change in temperature at sundown, nor the black fly slicing his ear lobe with microscopic precision. He does not hear the raven croaking in the top of a nearby spruce. His world is tunneled into a dimple on the surface of the water, into which tumble worries about the stock market, guilt about his recent divorce, and anxieties over work left undone. They will return, but their importance will be surprisingly diminished by this single evening.

Finally, he must look up because staring at the moving water has made him dizzy. When he shifts his gaze, the tree line seems to ripple against the sky, as if all things around him have turned into trout streams.

Then his eye is caught by a figure in the tail of the pool below him.

The angler is a woman, not a common sight alone in a trout stream at dusk, but more extraordinary is her casting. The young man would have to practice hard for ten years to approach her skill. The line straightens behind her, absolutely horizontal to the water, hovers for an instant, and then with line speed so quick you could not have separated the parts of the cast to analyze them, appears in front of her in a parabola that unrolls six inches from the water. The fly and leader settle to the water lightly, as if the woman has walked over to a place 60 feet away and dropped them from her hand.

Her ease with the fly rod is not innate. Although city-bound for months at a time as a surgeon in San Francisco, she casts a fly rod at least ten hours a week at the Golden Gate Casting Club. There she discovered how West Coast fishermen took a skill that eastern fishermen had used without a thought for improvement for generations and turned it into a sport.

The doctor was not born into a fly-fishing family, nor did she begin with the calculated idea of developing a hobby. Scheduled to attend a medical conference in Jackson, Wyoming, and ready to stretch it into a vacation, she studied tourist brochures and was intrigued by trout fishing, of which she knew nothing. She signed up for a fly-fishing school at a ranch in southern Oregon, located on a pair of small, clear, and productive spring creeks. She learned quickly.

Over the past 15 years she had driven a car infrequently, but had rented one for the trip to the school, and had spent the drive up edgy and tense, remembering why she so detested automobiles. On the way home, however, she found herself coasting along, humming Mozart, whistling Haydn, finally yelling Tchaikovsky melodies along with the radio. The sensuousness of fly-fishing had reawakened something in her.

At first, it was only the casting. Unlike other people who claimed they didn't need to catch fish to have a good time, she really did not. As much as the young man mesmerized himself with rises, she slipped away into the rhythm of casting and caught fish because when she did notice a trout rise, she could drill a fly into a spot the size of a coffee cup from as far away as she wished.

The doctor would not have understood the young man's fascination with flies and their construction. In fact, she would have laughed at his quest for the perfect blue dun rooster cape to match the color of a certain mayfly's wing, a color that eluded manmade dyes. To the doctor, flies were bought on the spot, like popcorn at the theater. She would stop at the nearest fly shop, throw herself at the mercy of the person behind the counter, use as many as she could on the trip, and then give them away before she left.

On this June evening, she uses an Ausable Wulff, a bushy, fast-water fly with white wings that she can locate amidst the flecks of foam, even 60 feet away. The man in the fly shop in Lake Placid told her that it would do a nice job of imitating the subimago of *Ephemera guttulatta*; the doctor gave him a patient smile and bought a dozen. Next month she will have forgotten the fly's name.

Despite her lack of interest in the trappings of the modern fly-fisherman, the doctor is intrigued by the history of the sport. Initially, she was attracted by its British aura, drawn to pictures in old books and magazines of men dressed in tweeds and bowler hats, plying the trout streams of Victorian England. Later, she was fascinated to read that fishing with an artificial fly was practiced over 2,000 years ago by the Macedonians, and was being written about in Spain, Germany, and France at least as early as the 13th century.

As the doctor fished a river, she liked to imagine the fly-fishermen who had waded the waters before her. On the Ausable, the first were probably British officers, traveling down Lake Champlain through Lake George and down the Hudson in the early 1700s. Part of a surveying party looking for the best route from Montreal to New York, they might have stopped at the mouth of the Ausable and found Atlantic salmon running the river to spawn.

In the middle of the next century, people from cities to the south like Boston and New York flocked to the Adirondacks. The first, from the emerging middle class, lived in tent camps and caught brook trout on lines rigged with as many as ten flies. They were considered idlers by most, as fishing in the 1850s was usually lumped with horse racing and cockfights. Later, wealthy industrialists built opulent hotels and casinos on what were once remote lakes, their private railroad cars, gleaming with brass and mahogany, arriving on spur lines right to the doorsteps of their lodges.

As the last light fades, the doctor imagines the man upstream dressed in the straw hat, heavy leather brogues, and rubberized canvas wading pants of 100 years ago.

Her reverie snaps as the young man hooks a trout; it is a rainbow of about 13 inches, and before he is through, he will catch two smaller rainbows and a brown trout. Despite the fact that the other two fishermen in the pool use different flies and have contrary approaches to fly-fishing, they also catch the same number of fish in about the same sizes.

Outside a streamside tavern, under neon beer advertisements, hangs a blackboard that gives current stream conditions and the flies that have caught the most fish that day. As the doctor stands outside reading the names of flies that mean nothing to her, she notices a young man creeping along the side of the brightly lit building, bobbing his head up and down and swiping the air with a cupped hand. She knows he is looking for mayflies attracted to the light. The man is oblivious to the diners on the other side of the picture window, but she can see that his pantomimes are making his audience uneasy. The doctor, however, senses a kindred soul, and she invites him inside for a drink.

Although tourists crowd the dining room, the bar is nearly empty. They sit and trade names and residences: David from Westport and Jean from San Francisco. The usual small talk about the evening hatch follows, and the conversation leads gradually into the gentle game of one-upmanship that fly-fishermen play: Where have you been?

"I have a lot of trouble going trout fishing after I get back from tarpon fishing in the Keys," David says. "It's hard to get excited about a 12-inch trout after playing a 100-pound tarpon. You see a vague gray shape in the water, you cast to it, and if the fish takes, you lose a couple seconds of your life. You can't remember a damn thing except the fly line disappearing like flash paper."

Jean can see nothing interesting about playing an oversized herring for hours while your arms ache, even if the toil is punctuated by a leap now and then. "Why do you even bother trout fishing?" she asks. "If you get that excited about big fish, how do you readjust?"

"It's hard at first, and then I start to remember the things that got me into trout fishing in the first place. Trying to match an insect precisely, which you don't have in saltwater fishing. Delicate, almost effortless casts. And I like the sense of history that you can't get away from when you're trout fishing. Did I hear you say that you've fished the chalk streams?"

A few seats down the bar, dressed in a red-checked shirt and talking quietly to the bartender, is the old man who had been in the river just upstream of David and Jean. At first, he hears none of their conversation. A glance at their clothes makes him deaf, with the mixture of jealousy and contempt that people who have grown up in tourist towns reserve for any face they do not recognize. But the words "trout" and "fly line" wear down his defenses, normally as insoluble as the granite boulders in the Ausable. He slides over a couple of seats.

After offering to buy them beers, he introduces himself as Ed and listens intently as Jean talks about the historic chalk streams of England.

"Most Englishmen still fish in tweeds and regimental ties and knickers—they call them breeks over there—but you have to remember that stream trout fishing is very expensive in England. Although there is some public reservoir fishing, every trout stream in

England is privately owned. What the three of us did tonight, stopping along the road wherever we pleased, is a concept that is absolutely alien to a European.

"So it's mostly the wealthy who fish trout streams in England. You know, I didn't mind the expense so much because I was only going to do it once, and I was able to learn to fish where I could drive into the mountains to any stream I wanted. Imagine trying to learn fly-fishing when it costs you a hundred bucks a pop!

"The English manicure their streams, which I guess is natural when you put such a high price tag on fishing them. Some of their rivers are really irrigation canals that date back to Roman times—you can tell because the banks are higher than the surrounding land. They spend thousands of pounds a year to shore up the banks, and if the curve of a bank doesn't please a landowner, he'll change it."

"Are the streams crowded?" David asks.

"Not the private rivers, no. There are only so many rods allowed to fish each stretch of water on any given day. On waters that are owned by a syndicate of fishermen you have to reserve your fishing days at the beginning of the season. And if you're a tourist renting a beat, no one else is rented the same piece of water that day.

"But you do see people and houses and farms everywhere you fish because there just isn't much wilderness left in England, especially in the south, where the chalk streams are. They've integrated civilization and nature quite well, though, I guess because they've had 2,000 years' head start on us. It's hard to tell where the riverbank ends and the neighbor's rose garden begins."

Ed tilts his bottle toward Jean and says, "Along those lines, once I was visiting my cousin in Grand Rapids, Michigan. I heard they were catching big trout right in the middle of the city, so I went there one morning to see for myself. You wouldn't believe the lake trout and steelhead those guys were pulling in."

He tells them of his reluctance to wade out into the raging current below the Sixth Street Dam, especially when he saw 30 fishermen in the same pool. The waders he had borrowed from his cousin did not have felt soles, practically guaranteeing that he would take a spill in the gray November water. Besides, the dingy buildings that surrounded the river made him uneasy, as did the hundreds of cars on the freeways flanking it.

Finally, two husky guys convinced him to wade out to the center, where the fish were, by each clamping on to one of his elbows and steering him around deep holes.

He caught three big lake trout, fish that had run up from Lake Michigan to spawn. Unlike the lakers in the Adirondacks, trolled up from 60 feet of water on lead core line, these fish fought with all the quick strength of wild brown trout. He also hooked a very large steelhead, perhaps 15 pounds, that spun him around in the current and stripped 100 yards of line and backing off his reel before the hook pulled out. The whole crew below the dam cheered him on as he fought the fish and then groaned with him as his line came back slack.

Although Ed hated to have even one other fisherman around when he was fishing, there, in the middle of a city, it seemed appropriate. The camaraderie that had apparently built up among regulars in the big pool drew attention away from the malignancy that Ed saw in every city he had ever visited.

"I drive hundreds of miles to fish for trout or fly for four hours to fish for tarpon," David says, "and I've got to be crazy. There's a beach across the street from my house on Long Island Sound where I can catch striped bass and bluefish on a fly six months a year. Some of the bass are over 20 pounds."

Jean and Ed have begun to compare West Coast and Michigan steelhead and do not seem to hear David. He begins to think of a Fourth of July night a couple of years ago.

The evening before, walking on the beach, he had seen swirls off the end of a jetty. Some of them were as big as truck tires, rising at unhurried intervals, as though the predators underneath were confident of taking their prey without fear of anything else in the water. Returning at midnight and wading up to his waist in the dark surf, he waited for the change of tide to pin the baitfish in a corner and drive the bass into a feeding spree.

Stalking a striped bass in the dark seemed private and almost primal—the only connection between him and the fish was a tiny hook dressed with a half-dozen chicken feathers and two bunches of deer hair, tied to a piece of nylon not much thicker than a thread. But all around him was humanity. He could hear the hum of roads leading to Manhattan, not 50 miles away. Teen-

agers laughed on the beach and firecrackers popped in the distance. One of Bruce Springsteen's songs blared from a tinny car radio abused to its maximum range. Airplanes flew in seemingly random directions in the sky above the Sound.

While he waited for the bass to come in, he made hundreds of casts. Two different shifts of lovers came and went on the jetty, never suspecting his presence 50 yards away. Cast, shoot line. Strip. Strip. Strip. Six inches of line came in on each strip until he had retrieved 60 feet, his hands repeating the task over and over again. This work might have hypnotized him, but the smell of low tide, the moil of a million dead and living creatures, and the phosphorescence gleaming at his waist every time he moved kept him from drifting off and losing his reference to reality.

What invigorated him most, though, was the knowledge that sooner or later a gentle bump telegraphed through 40 feet of plastic-coated fly line and 9 feet of nylon leader would turn into a force strong enough to double over his graphite rod.

He never saw the fish, but he could tell they were bass, probably 20 or 30 by the sound. Time and again he cast to where he heard the school, but not once did he feel a touch. Then, at about 3:30 A.M., a fish took and just moved off, not with the screaming runs you read about in the outdoor magazines, but as if an old lady driving a Pinto was hooked to the end of his line.

At one time, the fish had all his fly line and nearly 200 yards of backing, but just as dawn crept into his bleary eyes, he landed the 30-pound striper. He was going to release the fish and was sorry he wouldn't have a photo of such a prize. His luck held, though, as an early jogger saw him struggling with the bass, ran to his house, and returned with a camera. The great fish was photographed in the warm light and gingerly released.

"Last call."

The bartender's bellow brings him back to the present, and the three walk from the bar, exchanging scribbled addresses and promising to keep in touch, but they will probably never see nor hear from one another again. The future will bring too many new rivers and oceans, too many new companions, and too many stories for them to become anything other than fleeting, but genuine friends.

South Island, New Zealand.

River Test, England.
(Right) Grey Ghost.

18

Many people think that Englishman Izaak Walton was the first to write about fly-fishing, but his 17th-century masterpiece, *The Compleat Angler,* appeared 1,400 years after Roman Claudius Aelianus's description of Macedonian "fisherfolk" who "wrap ruby-colored wool about their hooks, and wind about this wool two feathers, which grow under a cock's wattles and are the color of dark wax."

In ancient Macedonia, men tried to fool fish with flies, and recent discoveries suggest that fly-fishing thrived in Germany and Spain in medieval times, but most modern techniques and the code of ethics associated with the sport do come from England, just not from Walton.

Izaak Walton was not even a fly-fisherman. In fact, no mention of fly-fishing appeared in his book until the sixth edition; in 1676, he asked his friend Charles Cotton, a wealthy landowner and sportsman, to write a second part, *Being Instructions How to Angle for a Trout or Grayling in a Clear Stream.* Cotton included detailed flytying instructions and 65 fly patterns for use on the River Dove alone.

Cotton, in turn, was not the first English fly-fishing authority. Two hundred years before him, Dame Juliana Berners wrote the earliest known fly-fishing monograph. Dame Juliana, an English gentlewoman, perhaps of noble lineage, provided sophisticated rod-building and flytying instructions in *A Treatyse of Fysshynge Wyth an Angle,* part of *The Boke of Saint Albans.* She also advised keeping your shadow off the water to avoid frightening the fish, and explained how to make hooks from needles and how to dye horsehair for line, specifying 9 hairs for trout and 16 for salmon.

Mention fly-fishing today and most people still think of Britain. Even though fishing vests, cowboy hats, and polarized sunglasses have replaced tweed jackets, bowlers, and smelly pipes, there is still something subliminally Anglophilic about the art. Fly-fishing flowered in England, and until well into the 20th century, American anglers looked across the Atlantic for advances in flies, tackle, and philosophy.

American writers were apologetic about fishing on this side of the Atlantic for most of the 19th century. The great outdoor writer Frank Forester, in an appendix to the 1847 edition of *The Compleat Angler* (Walton's word was still gospel, even 200 years after he wrote), compared Long Island trout streams to the chalk streams of England, going so far as to point out that "an Englishman, a celebrated shot and angler" was the first to use a fly on Long Island waters. Around the turn of the century, however, American fly-tiers, rod builders, fishermen, and writers began to develop their own style and sense of tradition.

Today it seems that Americans have finally claimed a place in this sport's long tradition. On a recent trip to England, my wife and I had lunch with an English publisher who is also a dedicated fly-fisherman. I remarked on all the beautiful English and Scottish cane rods I had seen, and on my feeling barbaric to be fishing with a tar-black graphite rod.

"Don't be silly," he said. "In your country a bamboo fly rod is considered an affectation, showing off. Here we crank them out on a production line, and everybody has one. An American graphite rod is considered the epitome of tackle here; it costs twice as much and casts worlds better than our creaky old bamboo."

Ballynahinch River, Connemara, Ireland.

River Kennet, England.
(Right) Irishman William Blacker's flies, engraving, *Blacker's Art of Fly-Making,* 1855.

BLACKER'S ART OF FLY-MAKING.

Flies described in Catalogue
(exact size)

Sprake. Sc.

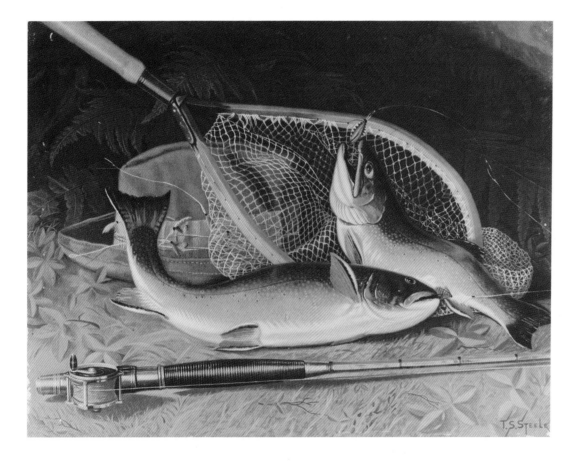

A Trout Pool on the Nepigon, engraving by H. Wolf after Hamilton, ca. 1890.
(Left) Two on a Cast, chromolithograph of an oil painting by T. S. Steele, 1903.

Salmon fishing, River Tay, Scotland.

Bonefishing, Christmas Island, Kiribati.
(Right) Laxa Blue.

28

 t the age of 20, I knew all I would ever need to know about casting. I was a real hotshot, a self-taught caster and flytier, highly regarded in the microcosm of the few trout streams near my home. Hearing about tournament fly-casting, I would say, "I'm a fisherman, not a caster. What do those guys who throw their flies into plastic hoops know about fishing, and who needs to be able to cast 100 feet, anyway? You can't hook a fish at that distance."

It took a trip to a sports show in San Francisco to make me realize what an inadequate caster I was. I saw a chubby little boy with red cheeks, no older than I was when I first picked up a fly rod, walk up to the casting platform and boom a whole fly line and about 20 feet of backing clear over the railing on the far side of the 90-foot pool.

Until that display I thought a cast was either bad or good, bad if the line didn't go where you wanted it to and good if it did. After five days of watching the casting pool at the sports show, it became obvious that even the mediocre casters there were years ahead of me. I had a lot to learn.

I now accept the fact that I will never be a great caster. You can practice eight hours a day for years, but the best fly-casters like many-times world champion Steve Rajeff have an unusual amount of strength and hand-eye coordination that come from genes, not practice. Even so, I intend to keep learning as long as my muscles and wrist hold up. One fact gives me hope—no cast is perfect. Each is as distinct as the spot pattern on a brown trout's back. As good as a cast looks, somewhere along that 70 feet of fly line and leader there will be a microscopic wrinkle.

Discovering that not all casting loops are the same, and that a tight one will let you throw more line with greater accuracy, I found that being able to cast a whole fly line made my 30-foot casts suddenly more precise. I began to enjoy those empty hours on the water when the fish were not feeding. Refining my casting skills opened a fresh source of pleasure that had been under my nose for years; I could feel the energy in my fingertips travel through the rod, out over the line, to the very tip of the leader.

This enlightened state gave me a new opinion of fly-fishing for salmon, steelhead, and striped bass, where you may have to cast for two days before you hook a fish. It is almost mandatory that you love the unfurling loops and the hoarse, whistling sound of your own casts when these fish are your quarry.

Best for those who enjoy casting, I think, is wet-fly fishing for Atlantic salmon. They are not very spooky, so you don't have to stalk them, and you can concentrate on your casting. You often must fish blind; a huge, unseen salmon may pass up your fly for 200 casts and take on number 201. Less air resistant than other types, salmon flies will not make a seemingly fluid cast suddenly dive to the right or left, as will bass bugs or big saltwater flies. So, you pick out a likely stretch of a secluded river and bang away, the allure being a combination of the scenery and the anticipation of a strike, but most of all, the increasingly smooth rhythm of your casting.

Many trout fishermen still use my old excuse, "I'm a fisherman, not a caster." Funny, but I've never heard those words on a salmon river.

Little Redfish Lake, Idaho.

Parachute casting for rainbow, Rivadavia River, Argentina.
(Left) Western Run, Maryland.

Hillside above Wenatchee River, Washington.
(Right) Fishing for cutthroat and bull trout, North Fork, Flathead River, Montana.

34

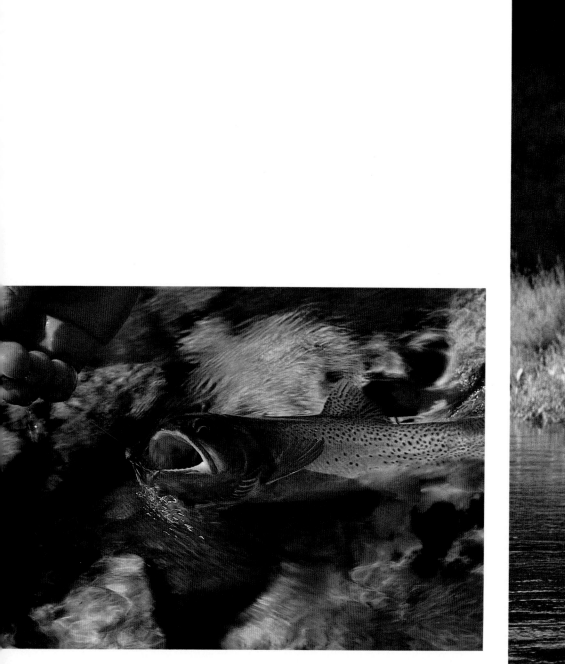

Depuy's Spring Creek, Montana.
(Left) Cutthroat trout, Yellowstone River, Yellowstone National Park, Wyoming.

Casting for bonefish, Christmas Island, Kiribati.

Choosing a smallmouth bass fly, Muddy Creek, Pennsylvania.
(Right) Flashy Pheasant Stonefly.

f you are a serious flytier, catching a fish on a store-bought fly is like shooting a grouse over someone else's dog— the motions are there, but you regret the final touch that would have made the whole achievement yours. Many times the store-bought fly might work better, but if I am offered a homemade fly by a friend or someone I meet while fishing, I accept it gratefully, try it out, and slip it into my vest. Later, it goes into The Fly Box.

The Fly Box is a large cardboard box full of hundreds of flies in smaller plastic boxes. It is a 20-year-old, completely unorganized collection. Most of the flies are unlabeled, but I know where each one came from and why it means something to me. A couple of times a year, usually in the winter and late at night when the family is in bed, I'll pull out The Box and, under a single light in my office, paw through it at random, quizzing myself on each fly's origin.

Many are from fishing buddies; I have tried to collect a fly from everyone with whom I have ever fished. One box is for flies found in trees and another for flies I have discovered in fish's mouths when extracting my fly to release them. When I am looking for new patterns to try, I pay more attention to the latter box.

Some are flies from Famous People. It is stupid of me not to get these documented, because I have seen a fly from a Famous Person (still living!) go for over $100 at a Trout Unlimited auction. One fly. But maybe I have subconsciously done this on purpose, so that it makes the collection worth nothing to anyone but me and the friends I wish to share it with.

Once I remarked to one of these friends that I thought Bill Hunter was the finest salmon-fly tier

around. He told Hunter, who then sent me a full-dress Atlantic salmon fly, a three-inch, double-hooked 6/0 that greets me when I first open The Box, its speckled Guinea fowl, waxy jungle cock, and shimmering golden pheasant tippets an evocation of Victorian England in yellows, blues, and greens.

Many of the flies are ones I have tied myself, kept in memory of a special event. A ragged Sulphur Spinner, almost destroyed by a fish, celebrates my first brown trout over 20 inches. In the same box is an Ausable Wulff that caught a 12-inch cutthroat, an absolutely insignificant event if it were not my first cutthroat ever and my first fish in Wyoming. I can still see exactly the way water ran against the undercut bank and what the rise looked like, and hear the whoops of a cowboy friend who had spent a year in Vermont as my roommate and was now returning the favor. Without that fly I would not have recalled a damn thing.

The most pragmatic reason for keeping The Fly Box is that it provides a three-dimensional file of flies from tiers whose style or patterns I admire. One tier's flies have received more attention than any other. He is not famous. In fact, he is a construction worker from upstate New York who drives one of those monstrous earth movers with tires as tall as I am. Del's hands would never be mistaken for those of a piano player, yet the classic Catskill-style dry flies that he ties are like no others. With the simple ingredients of fox fur, wood duck feathers, and blue dun rooster hackles, he can create the most delicate, tightly wound flies I have seen. I have yet to figure out how Del dubs his bodies so tightly, even after many phone calls to him, squinting at his flies with a hand lens while I listen. But if you think I'm going to cut one of his flies apart, you are crazy.

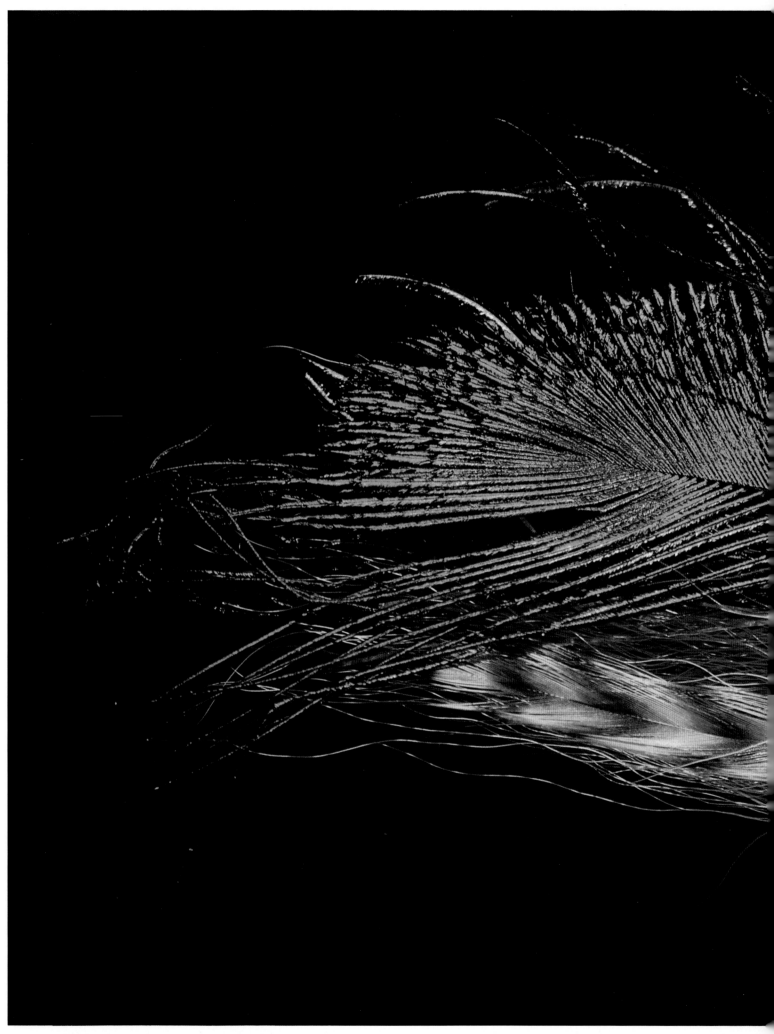

Bob Quigley's Yellow-Barred Yellow Streaker.

Spent mayflies caught in an eddy, Pere Marquette River, Michigan.
(Left) Mayfly hatch, Lake Murray, South Carolina.

(Upper) Green Drake mayfly examining its counterpart.

(Lower) Salmonfly nymph and its imitation, a Kaufmann's Stonefly.

Lee Wulff tying a White Wulff dry fly.

Surf fishing for trevally, Bay of Wrecks, Christmas Island, Kiribati.
(Left) Skipping Bugs used for baby tarpon.

Flies, including mouse flies, used in Alaska for salmon and rainbow.
(Right) Bonefishing gear.

Selecting a fly, Armstrong Spring Creek, Montana.
(Left) Wulff flies.

Playing a trout from a belly boat, Henry's Fork Reservoir, Idaho.
(Right) Black-Nosed Dace.

54

couple of years ago, several makers of high-quality fly reels estimated the size of the saltwater reel market, and they figured that there were three times as many reels sold as fishermen using them. Three-hundred-dollar reels do not wear out, and you can only use one at a time. So, many must sit on shelves, taken down only to hear the purr of their gears when the owner daydreams about the bonefish flats.

Bamboo fly rods are also becoming collectors' items. Most of the manufacturers of handmade bamboo rods have noted at least a modest increase in orders in the past five years—yet almost none of these are returning for repairs. Sales of graphite rods are booming, but these rods are coming back to the shop in numbers that suggest they are falling victim to screen doors, power windows, and streamside rocks.

Sportsmen, of course, have long been ridiculed for their tendency to accumulate devices they may never use. Cartoons from the 1920s portray fly-fishermen burdened with all kinds of Rube Goldberg contraptions. Most of the jokes are based on the theme of the little boy with a worm, stick, and bent pin selling a stringer of trout to a fat old man festooned with gear.

Today, self-appointed spokesmen for the fly-fishing world pontificate on just how many gadgets a fly-fisherman needs. Once a man wrote me to complain about the proliferation of doodads in the fly-fishing catalogues. He said that the sport was being ruined for him, and that he did not want to carry all that stuff in his vest. I asked him if he felt compelled to buy everything in a grocery store when he went in for a head of lettuce

Two of my friends represent the extremes in fly-fishing gear accumulation. One, a Vermont farm-er, uses an old fiberglass rod and three wet flies on droppers in the brook behind his house. A few days ago, stopping by to pick up a half-dozen ears of sweet corn, I saw his gear hanging from the rafters in his garage: one pair of hip boots and one rod, still strung with a Royal Coachman, Black Gnat, and a Hare's Ear. He needs no dry-fly spray because he does not fish with dries, no leader wallet or tippet spools because his leaders are so heavy they never break, no fly boxes because he never uses any other flies.

My other friend has spent the last 20 years as a photojournalist. His fishing vest is as heavy as a golf bag full of clubs, and you never know what he might pull out of it—a collapsible insect net that can reach 15 feet out into a river, a box full of tarpon flies (this on a small Vermont brook trout stream), four different kinds of dry-fly spray, pliers, forceps, two flashlights—everything except camera equipment, which I've never seen him carry.

On a fishing trip, we have to blindfold him when we pass a tackle shop. If there is no tackle shop in town, he has been known to settle for a hardware store. It takes hours to get him out, much to the aggravation of the other people riding with him, who would like to spend those hours on a trout stream before it gets dark.

On a recent pass through town, he dragged me from the office and into the back of his old VW van, which houses about 30 large Tupperware containers of flytying gear. Like a kid showing off a birthday present, he pulled out his newest purchase. It seems he was in Thailand on assignment and had noticed some men fishing in the canals. Of course, his first question after asking about their luck that day was, "Where did you get that gear?"

He bought two homemade crossbows.

Minipi Lake, Newfoundland, Canada.

Trout stream, Olympic National Park, Washington.
(Upper left) Releasing a rainbow, Loving Creek, Idaho.
(Lower left) Double Egg Sperm Fly and reel.

Running Buckskin Mary Rapids during June salmonfly hatch, Deschutes River, Oregon.
(Left) Camp, Deschutes River.

Rappahannock River, Virginia.
(Right) Gear, wilderness float trip, Chosen River, Alaska.

Loading float planes, Naknek River, Alaska.
(Left) Netting a rainbow, Grindstone Lake, Oregon.

Rainbow, Madison River, Yellowstone National Park, Wyoming.
(Right) Light Cahill.

Today's fly-fishermen are true pioneers, because we are just beginning to explore the great variety of species we can catch with a fly rod.

There is a lot of talk about the recent revolution in fly-rodding for bass, but I think it is more of a resurgence. Americans have fished for largemouth and smallmouth bass with a fly rod since this continent was first settled. One hundred years ago they were creating fly patterns specifically for bass; Mary Orvis Marbury, in her 1893 classic *Famous Flies,* lists 58 bass flies and provides full-color illustrations. Fly-fishing was only eclipsed by the novelty of spin fishing when that method was introduced from Europe after World War II.

Freshwater fish like bass are old quarry, and these days saltwater species like bonefish and tarpon are considered standard fly-rod species. We are pushing the frontier, discovering that saltwater fish previously considered bait or trash species are challenging game on a fly rod. Barracuda have saved the day for many fishermen when a cold front sent the more sensitive bonefish into deep water. Bonito, small relatives of tuna used for bait by bluewater fishermen, are tremendous battlers on light fly rods and can be as choosy as trout. Some fishermen claim bonito strip line off a reel faster than bonefish.

It is freshwater trash fish that really interest me, though. Many of them take flies, and not all call for subsurface fishing. For a few weeks in August every year, a mayfly hatch of the species *Ephoron* blankets the surface of many large rivers in the Northeast. Most often fishermen associate this hatch with trout and smallmouth bass, but some of my friends in Vermont and Pennsylvania have even caught wall-

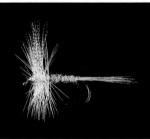

eyes and channel catfish on dry flies during this feeding spree.

Carp, the ultimate trash fish, are selective and spooky, traits usually associated with brown trout, and they grow regularly to over 20 pounds within the city limits of most metropolitan areas. They take nymphs and streamers well, and I can guarantee that you will not have any competition—fly-fishermen like their fish pretty or not at all.

I was introduced to carp on a bass-fishing trip to Florida; the bass had just finished spawning, and the barometer had taken a nose dive, so the fish were sulking in deep water—too deep to take them comfortably with a fly rod. My fishing buddy, who is a fisheries biologist, took me to a nearby two-acre pond to show me what the introduction of grass carp had done. All the other ponds in the area had been choked with weeds, but the carp had removed every bit of vegetation from this one in a matter of months.

With a gleam in his eye, my friend happened to mention that grass carp become insectivores after they eat all the vegetation, so I cast a tiny bluegill bug into the center of the pond and let it sit. In 30 seconds, a long, dark shape slid under the fly and hung with its nose just a half inch below the surface. I gave the fly a small twitch, and the fish inhaled it in slow motion, majestic as any rise I have seen in a Paradise Valley spring creek. That carp was not a shabby fighter either and used all of his ten pounds in an attempt to burn out the drag on my reel.

I have heard about a group of fishermen in Houston who chum grass carp close to shore with grass clippings they get from golf courses, and then fish for the carp with green marabou streamers. As soon as I get an invitation, I'm packing my bags.

Cradling a rainbow before release, Silver Creek, Idaho.

Releasing a steelhead, Babine River, British Columbia, Canada.
(Right) Spawning sockeye salmon, Copper River, Alaska.

Barracuda, Los Roques Islands, Lesser Antilles, Venezuela.

Bonefish, Turneffe Islands, Belize.

Arctic grayling on an egg fly, Naknek River, Alaska.

Tarpon hooked on a Lefty's Deceiver, Placentia Point, Belize.

(Above and left) Northern pike fishing with streamer flies, Okstukuk Lake, Alaska.

Guide displaying Arctic char, Coppermine River, Northwest Territories, Canada.
(Right) Smallmouth bass caught with a Keel Fly Streamer, Susquehanna River, Pennsylvania.

Brook trout, Eagle River, Newfoundland, Canada.

Fishing for rainbow, Upper Mesa Falls, Henry's Fork, Snake River, Idaho.
(Right) T.R. Shad Fly.

82

PLACES

cenery. What an inadequate word for the reason many of us fish. I love to watch a fly-fisherman's reaction when he first glimpses Montana as we drive away from the Bozeman airport, and his gradual seduction as we head out of the dry farm country into the chilly, all-day shade of the Gallatin Canyon.

After we have caught a few small rainbows in the Gallatin to pacify our casting arms, which have twitched involuntarily with the sight of each delicious pool along the river, we might drive over to Paradise Valley, the valley of the lower Yellowstone. Here, instead of hemming us in with canyon walls, the mountains stand back, as if fearing to smother the delicate spring creeks. When you first stand on the bluffs overlooking the springs, it is almost shocking to see them so full of bright green plant life, when the surrounding land is a dusty tan and the air sometimes heavy with the smell of forest fires.

Have you ever looked at the rocks on river bottoms, really looked at them and studied the textures and colors and the way sand and algae add bright highlights? I have. In fact, I've collected rocks from every stream I have ever fished and photographed most of them—try explaining this part of your photo album.

There are two small trout streams within walking distance of my house. Both arise in the same mountain range, and both have about the same flow, yet they are as different as fraternal twins. Many flat rocks, almost slabs, cover the bed of the one across the street. Most of them are a rusty yellow color. I feel a special kinship to this stream because the quartzite on its bed is exactly the same as that in the rocks in the foundation of my 200-year-old house. The solid, stable character this bottom lends to the stream seems to be reflected in its abundant aquatic life.

The one beyond the field in the back of my house is a volatile brother, with a black and pink and white bottom of rounded pebble- to pumpkin-sized gneiss that rumbles and crunches with every spring flood. This stream holds little attraction for brook trout larger than six inches.

A little farther down the road is the Battenkill, with one of the finest palettes that ever graced a trout stream: black against white marble, with sparkles of mica thrown in, and bluish slate every few feet adding a primary color. Yet, even though my other two streams are tributaries of the Battenkill, I see little of their bottom signatures on the larger river.

I have made my own regional bottom classifications as well. Pennsylvania streams have dusky shale and limestone, and a fossil or two if you look closely enough. Many of the Idaho rivers like the Fall and Henry's Fork are made up of a rough, black rock, basalt, I believe, and I cannot see this rock anywhere without thinking of fat rainbow trout. The Madison has flowery pink, black, and white granite, as if to make up for the thirsty rangeland that surrounds the lower river. I remember lying on a gravel bar in Alaska, sifting pebbles through my fingers and wondering if I had ever seen a bottom with so many green rocks. I like to think it was jade that came back in a pocket of my fishing vest, but I haven't gotten around to asking someone who knows about rocks; I would just be disappointed.

The only place I have ever fished that did not provide me with a rock was Christmas Island. The largest coral atoll in the world, it does not have any, and I had to settle for some pieces of coral I found on the beach.

Okstukuk Lake, Alaska.

(Above and right) San Pedro, Belize.

86

Fishing for winter salmon, South Fork, Eel River, California.

Casting for brown trout, Green Spring Run, Pennsylvania.
(Right) Purple loosestrife, Housatonic River, Connecticut.

Silver Creek, Idaho.

Midway Geiser Basin, Firehole River, Yellowstone National Park, Wyoming.

Beaverkill River, New York.
(Left) Naud Lake, Michigan.

97

Taking a break, Cline Falls, Deschutes River, Oregon.
(Left) Lower Falls, Yellowstone River, Yellowstone National Park, Wyoming.

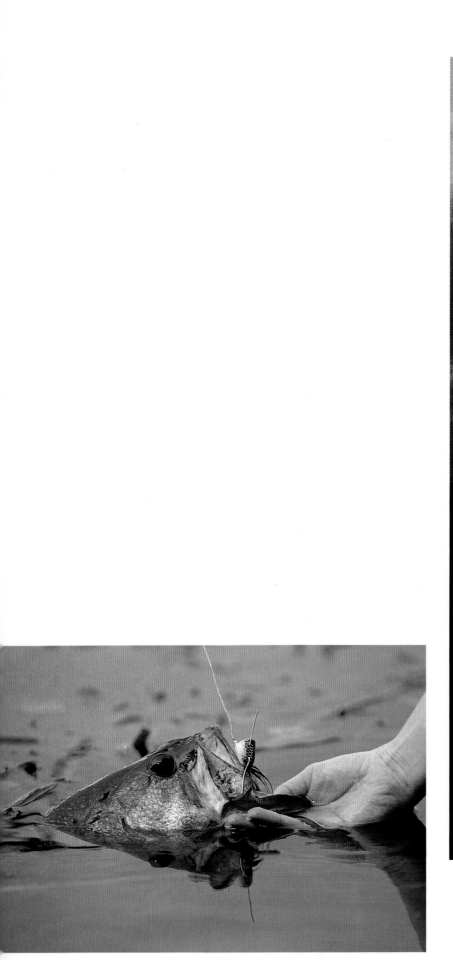

Bass fishing from an airboat, Everglades, Florida.
(Left) Landing a largemouth bass caught on a Black Popper, St. Johns River, Florida.

Sogne Fjord, Norway.

Poling in the shallows for bonefish, Boca Paila, Yucatan, Mexico.
(Right) Blue Marabou.

One reason fly-fishing appeals to sportsmen is that it incorporates many of the elements of hunting. If you could merely walk up to a fish, cast, and catch it without planning your position, you might as well stay home and watch bowling. Fly-fishermen and hunters know that some quarry call for a more careful stalk than others. Anglers often speak of the challenges presented by the neurotic tendencies of bonefish and brown trout, but over the past decade I have come to respect one fish usually thought of as a pushover—the cutthroat trout.

Anyone who backpacks into the Rocky Mountains and fishes a wilderness lake can probably substantiate the stories of the Yellowstone cutthroat's brainless abandon in taking the fly. The tough ones, however, are the fine-spotted Snake River cutthroat, a subspecies that seems to possess all the slyness of a Battenkill brown or a Henry's Fork rainbow. You won't find them in just any body of water, though; the fish that live in the mainstream of rivers like the Snake or Salt seem to be as gullible as their relatives to the north. The cutthroat that have driven me to believe I am a complete clod live in the diminutive, spring-fed tributaries of these river systems.

Hike into a meadow with the glacier-clad Tetons towering impossibly high above it, approach one of these tributaries, and from 100 feet away you will spot broad heads poking through the surface film, sipping tiny insects off the water. As you get closer, their vermillion gill covers and golden yellow flanks assure you that they are cutthroat, and that pickings will be easy. You move near one pod of three or four fish, however, and they bolt, flushing upstream and down, leaving only smooth wakes behind them.

You soon learn how spooky they can be. You look carefully for another pod of fish, approaching from downstream so that you are invisible to them. Kneeling to keep your profile low, you watch them feeding confidently, tipping their heads up so frequently that they appear to be using aquatic trampolines. Pick the closest fish; this is not a time to flock-shoot. He has a metronomic rhythm, one rise every three seconds, and you time your cast to put the fly over his head just before a rise. The rise does not happen, though, and the cutthroat hangs suspended under the surface, as if he were waiting for your fly to get out of the way.

One minute later the fish feeds again, but this time your cast lands too hard and really scares him. He streaks upstream to find a safer spot, but the place he wants to be is already occupied by another trout, and they whirl around each other briefly until your friend gets his way and chases his rival further upstream. You look for another fish to cast to and find one 20 feet away, directly across the stream from you. Wait. Watch this one for a minute so that you do not make the same mistake. Suddenly, out of the corner of your eye, you catch a wink on the surface upstream, and as you turn your head, you discover the first fish back in his original position.

You decide to try another fly and tie on a shiny Pheasant Tail nymph. Pitching it upstream to the first fish, you are careful to cast to the trout's near side to avoid placing the leader over his nose. He moves toward the nymph, follows it two feet downstream, but then turns away without inhaling the fly. Cast again. This time a gust of wind blows your leader on top of his head. The fish turns and swims downstream, and with an arrogant flip of his tail swims right past you, so close you could poke him with your rod tip. As he passes, he sips an insect on the run, lordly behavior for a supposedly stupid fish.

Nymph fishing, DePuy's Spring Creek, Montana.

Waiting for a hatch of mayfly duns, Thousand Springs, Idaho.
(Left) Brown bear eyeing a salmon run, Katmai National Park, Alaska.

Dropping a dry fly near a rising trout, Spruce Creek, Pennsylvania.
(Left) Fishing for rainbow, Salmon River, Idaho.

Silver Creek, Idaho.

Stalking cutthroat in pocket water, North Fork, Blackfoot River, Montana.
(Left) Winter nymph fishing, Big Hunting Creek, Maryland.

Guide pointing out a bonefish, Andros Island, Bahamas.

*I*t has always annoyed me that most non-fishers think fly-fishing is just playing a fish, banging it on the head, and slipping it into a frying pan. And it does nothing for your standing with future in-laws or business clients when you tell them you fish for eight-inch brook trout, which hardly put a bend in a rod, and release all of them unharmed. "Oh, you just do it for the sport," is the way they usually back out of the conversation, with a tone that suggests that they have filed you away with the fellow they met last week who was lining up 10,000 dominoes in order to make the record books.

Once in a while you will get someone to hang around long enough for you to tell him that two of the most exciting fish you can catch on a fly rod—tarpon and bonefish—are inedible. I have to confess, though, that I am beginning to doubt this one. When I was on Christmas Island, a Japanese fisherman who took great delight

in preparing delicious fish cakes did not tell the American tourists until after dinner that they had eaten bonefish. I have never heard of anyone eating tarpon, but maybe this story of inedible game-fish was started by some clever guide who wanted to protect a limited resource. I sometimes wish colonial fly-fishermen had lied 200 years ago about the tastiness of salmon.

It is the strike that keeps most anglers coming back. Think about those events that give a fly-fisherman tingles years after they have occurred: bonefish nosing through ankle-deep transparent water, brown trout rising to mayflies in spring creeks, a bass taking a popper on the shiny surface of a pond at dawn. Although some of the strikes, espe-cially the brown and the bonefish, hardly take with a magazine-cover splash, the moment just before the fish inhales the fly causes a rush of adrenalin.

Many fly-fishermen in the middle of a heavy insect hatch with trout rising all around them will look for another fish as they are playing one, and may shake a small fish off or even break one off so that they do not waste any time. A Montana fishing guide told me about a woman who always brought two completely rigged rods into the drift boat with her. When she hooked a trout, she immed-iately handed the rod to the guide and began cast-ing for another fish.

I will still play the game when the quarry makes up for it with a fight that I have a chance of losing. For example, I have fished for steelhead using long leaders loaded with lead shot, where casting is neither pretty nor particularly safe. The strike is merely a slight pause in the down-stream movement of the line. But when a steelhead leaves the water, returns twice before I can react in any rational manner, then yanks the rod parallel to the surface, spins 50 yards of line from my reel, and wraps me around a submerged willow root, it deserves attention.

I have heard of places in Costa Rica where it is worth your while to hang a fly in coffee-colored currents on a fast-sinking line and just wait. If you can stand the inactivity, sooner or later an 80-pound tarpon will grab the fly, and tear up the water, your tackle, and your shoulder muscles. This sort of fish-ing is scorned by the Florida clear-water flats fisher-men, who stalk their fish for hours, sometimes casting only a couple of times a day.

I don't think I'll live long enough to get that proud.

Playing a rainbow, Deschutes River, Oregon.

Largemouth bass *(above)* approaching a Whitfrog fly, and *(right)* leaping, hooked on a popper, Lake Okeechobee, Florida.

Fighting a king salmon, Nushagak River, Alaska.

(Right) Hooking a rainbow, Shelter Lake, British Columbia.

Catching bonefish, *(above)* Key Largo, Florida, and *(left)* Turneffe Islands, Belize.

Angler's first Atlantic salmon, Gaula River, Norway.
(Left) Forty-five-pound salmon, Gaula River.

DePuy's Spring Creek, Montana.

Henry's Fork, Snake River, Idaho.
(Right) Purple Dahlberg Diver.

*P*assions for fly-fishing run so high that friendships made on the water seldom wane, even after both parties have been separated by years and miles. Although one of the finest things that can happen to a fly-fisherman is to discover a pool full of rising trout with no one else around, it is even better to return to the same pool later and share it with a good friend.

Fishing partners have to be chosen carefully. Can he or she get up at the crack of dawn without grumbling just to see the first light touch the water, even though the fishing might not be any good until the afternoon? Will there be tense moments when one of you catches a fish on every cast, while the other goes fishless for hours? Do you really want a partner who has to stop for silly things like lunch, dinner, and, for God's sake, cocktails at five?

It is hard to find a true fishing buddy and even harder to lose one.

One of the first times I saw Tony was in the Marble Pool on the Battenkill. A figure in the evening light ahead of me kept hooking fish, big ones by the look of the bend in his rod. I would have been yelling my head off, but I could tell by his calm body language that such success happened to him every day.

Although time and emotion cloud my perception of his abilities, I still think of Tony as one of the best fishermen and flytiers I ever knew, and the only person with whom I could share a horribly disappointing day of fishing followed by a night in a soggy tent and still be laughing the next morning.

His most annoying habit was also the idiosyncracy that made him such a great fisherman. Tony could not pass up a rising fish. He would cast to a tiny brook trout for an hour, even if there were plenty of bigger ones feeding a few yards upstream.

Let's face it—fishing is playing. Because both of us had made fly-fishing our careers as well as our pastimes, we were not emotionally prepared for the news that put an end to our fun. Before he was diagnosed as having terminal lymphoma, neither of us had ever worried too much about mortality, although I could see it in his eyes at the end.

On the opening day of trout season in April, a month after he died, our friend John and I waded out into the Marble Pool to scatter Tony's ashes. Our wives, Tony's widow Lynn, her parents, and Tony's son Lance waited on the bank. Mayflies were rising from the surface as his remains fell to meet them. I had expected the ashes to be in an urn, but they were in a plastic bag inside a plain cardboard box, so I was glad we had brought flowers to throw in as well. It was the only time I have ever cried while wearing waders. Later that day I fished 10 miles downstream, hoping, I guess, for something poetic to happen. I imagined I would see the white flowers floating toward me, and right in the middle of the bouquets a giant brown trout would rise up to snatch my fly. As I remember, it was an uneventful afternoon.

For three years, I avoided the Marble Pool. When I finally decided to fish there, I was not expecting anything like a sign from heaven, but hoped I might hook one of those big browns Tony seduced so easily. This did not happen, but every good spot gave up a small trout, little brookies and browns, none of them longer than my nine-inch hand-span. I fished for each yearling as if it were the last one I would ever see.

Fishing the evening hatch for brown trout, Misty River, South Island, New Zealand.

Sizing up an Arctic char, Ugashik Narrows, Alaska.
(Right) Guide and ranch caretaker, Fall River, California.

Atlantic salmon fishing, Laxa i Adaldal, Iceland.

Lake Aleknagik, Alaska.

Henry's Fork, Snake River, Idaho.

Releasing a brown trout, Big Horn River, Montana.

P H O T O G R A P H Y   C R E D I T S